KU-161-054

WS 2252767 2

S-2008

For Tina - H.B.
For my family and friends - R. D.

Mantra Lingua Ltd
Global House, 303 Ballards Lane, London N12 8NP
www.mantralingua.com

First published in 2002 by Mantra Lingua Ltd
This edition 2007
Text & Illustrations copyright © 2002 Mantra Lingua
-All rights reserved

A CIP record for this book is available from the British Library

CR
P
BIAR

ال ـ پيد پايپر

The Pied Piper

retold by Henriette Barkow
illustrated by Roland Dry

Arabic translation by Dr. Sajida Fawzi

mantra lingua

يعتقد البعض أن هذه القصة حقيقية ويعتقد البعض الآخر أنها ليست حقيقية.
ولكن في كلا الحالتين فسأحكي لكم هذه القصة.
من سنين مضت في الزمان القديم كان هناك مدينة تعرف بإسم هاملِن.
وكانت هاملِن مدينة عاديّة ويسكنها ناس عاديّون مثلي ومثلك.
وفي إحدى السنين اجتاحت الفئران هذه المدينة. فكان هناك فئران كبيرة وأخرى صغيرة
وكان بعضها سميناً وبعضها الآخر كان ضعيفاً أينما تنظر تجد فئران!

Some people believe this story is true, and others that it is not. But either way this story I will tell to you.

Many years ago, in the days of old, there was a town called Hamelin. It was an ordinary town, with ordinary people just like you and me.

One year the town had an invasion of RATS. There were big rats and small rats, fat rats and thin rats. Wherever you looked there were RATS!

وكما تتصور فقد أزعج هذا الوضع سكّان المدينة فهبّوا متوجهين إلى دار البلدية وطالبوا العُمدة أن يفعل شيئاً.

"ماذا تتوقعون مني أن أفعل؟ أنا لست صيّادفئران!" صرخ العُمدة.

As you can imagine, the people of the town were very upset. They stormed to the town hall and demanded that the mayor do something.
"What do you expect me to do?" he shouted. "I'm not a rat catcher!"

وفي تلك اللحظة ظهر شخص غريب يرتدي ملابس غريبة جداً ويمسك بيده مزمار. وأطال الناس النظر اليه كما كانوا يفعلون عادة مع الغرباء ولكن يبدو أن ذلك لم يزعجه.

At that very moment a stranger appeared, wearing the most unusual clothes and holding a pipe in his hand. The crowd stared at the stranger, the way that people often stare at strangers, but that didn't bother him.

توجه هذاالرجل الغريب نحو العُمدة مباشرة وقدّم نفسه اليه قائلاً " يعرفني الجميع باء سم ال ـ بيد پايپر
وباءمكاني أن أخلصكم من كل فئرانكم إذا كنت مستعداً أن تدفع لي عشرين قطعة من الذهب."
إستحسن العُمدة هذا الكلام " إن كنت فعلاً ستحقق ما قلته، فيسعدني جداً أن أ دفع لك المبلغ"
أجاب العُمدة.

The stranger walked straight up to the mayor and introduced himself. "They call me the
Pied Piper and if you pay me twenty pieces of gold I will take all your rats away."
Well this was music to the mayor's ears. "If you can truly do what you say, I shall be more
than happy to pay you," he replied.

وكان سكان المدينة يراقبون وينتظرون ماذا سيحصل. هل هذا الرجل الذي يطلَق عليه بيد بايبر سيستطيع حقاً أن يقضي على كل الفئران الصغيرة الحجم والكبيرة والصغيرة العمر والكبيرة؟

The town's people waited and watched. Could this so called Pied Piper really get rid of all the rats - the big rats and the small rats, the young rats and the old rats?

وبدأ ال ـ پيد پايپر يُزمّر بمزماره بهدوء وفجأة حدث أمر لا يصدّق. فقد خرجت الفئران من كل ركن وشق متّجهة إلى الشارع وتبعت ال ـ پايپر على أ نغام الموسيقى.

The Pied Piper slowly started to play his pipe and an unbelievable thing happened. From every nook and cranny the rats poured out onto the street, and under the spell of the music, they followed the piper.

تبعته الفئران خارج مدينة هاملِن بإتجاه نهر ڤيسَر. وهنا غيّر ال ـ پيد پايپِر
النغمة إلى لحن حزين باك. وإذا بالفئران ترمي
بنفسها إلى ماء النهر القارس البرد وتغرق.

They followed him out of Hamelin town to the river Weser. Here, the Pied Piper
changed his tune and with a mournful wailing, the rats threw themselves into the
icy water and drowned.

وكان العمدة مدينة هاملِن رجل طمّاع ولم يكن يفكر ليعطي إيّ مال لِرجل غريب.
وعندما جاء ال ـ بيد پايپر يطالِب العمدة بقطع النقود الذهبية ضحك العمدة وهزَّ رأسه
"الآن وقد تخلصنا من الفئران فلِمَ أعطيك أي شيئ ؟" أجاب العمدة مكشّراً.

Now the mayor of Hamelin was a greedy man, and he wasn't going to
give any money to a stranger. When the Pied Piper came and demanded his
pieces of gold the mayor laughed and shook his head. "Now that the rats
are gone why should I give you anything?" he snarled.

وقف الناس يستمعون . ورغم أنهم يعلمون أن العمدة كان خاطئاً في كلامه
ولكنهم لم يساندوا ال ـ بايبر ولم يفتحوا فمهم ولا حتى بكلمة واحدة.

The people stood and listened. They didn't stand up for
the piper, even though they knew that their mayor was wrong.
They didn't say a word.

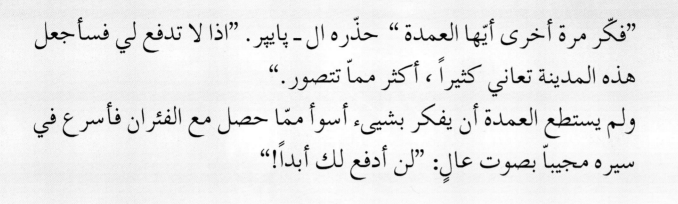

"فكّر مرة أخرى أيّها العمدة " حذّره ال ـ پايپير . "اذا لا تدفع لي فسأجعل هذه المدينة تعاني كثيراً، أكثر ممّا تتصور."

ولم يستطع العمدة أن يفكر بشيىء أسوأ ممّا حصل مع الفئران فأسرع في سيره مجيباً بصوت عالٍ: "لن أدفع لك أبداً!"

"Think again, mayor!" the piper warned. "If you don't pay, then I will make this town suffer more than you can ever imagine."

Well the mayor couldn't think of anything worse than the rats and so he stomped off shouting: "I WILL NEVER PAY YOU!"

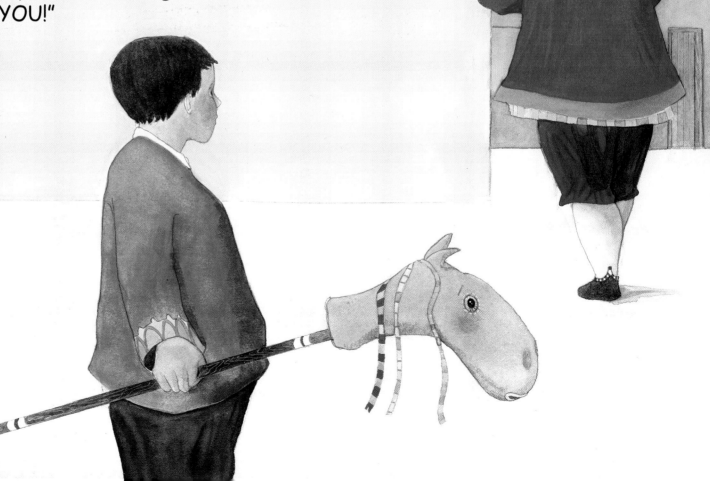

وفي عصر نفس اليوم وبينما كان الناس مشغولين بتصليح مدينتهم ، وقف
الـ ـ پيد پايپر في ساحة المدينة. رفع المزمار ببطيء إلى شفتيه
وعزف لحناً تعجز الكلمات عن وصفه.

That very afternoon, while the people were busy repairing their
town, the Pied Piper stood in the town square. Slowly he lifted the
pipe to his lips, and played a tune that no words could describe.

وعلى كل لحن جديد تجمّع عدد أكثر وأكثر من الأطفال يرقصون
ويغنّون على أنغام الموسيقى .

With each new note more and more children appeared,
and danced and sang to the music.

واستدار ال ـ پيد پايپر متجهاً خارج المدينة وتبعه
الأطفال متأثّرين بسحر الموسيقى.

The Pied Piper turned and walked out of the town playing his
pipe and all the children followed, caught under the
spell of his music.

وعلى قمة التل رقصوا وغنّوا على ألحان الموسيقى.
وعندما أوشكوا على ألّا نتهاء انفتح باب أمامهم.

Up the hill they danced and sang to the rhythm of the tune. When it looked like they could go no further, a door opened before them.

وتبعوا ال ـ بيد پايپر واحداً واحداً إلى داخل التل من غير عودة.
دخلوا كلّهم إلا واحداً فلم يستطع أن يلحق بالآخرين.

One by one the children followed the Pied Piper into the heart of
the hill forever. All except one, who could not keep up with the others.

عاد الطفل الصغير إلى المدينة وكأن عودته أزالت السحر عنها.

ونظر الناس إليه غير مصدقين عندما أخبرهم بما حدث.

فبكوا على أطفالهم ونادوا عليهم ولكن لم يروهم مرة أخرى.

When the little boy returned to the town it was as if a spell had been broken.
The people stared at him in disbelief when he told them what had happened.
They called and cried for their children, but they never saw them again.

Key Words

town	مدينة
people	ناس
rats	فئران
town hall	دار البلدية
mayor	العمدة
rat catcher	صيّاد الفئران
stranger	غريب
clothes	ملابس
pipe	مزمار
crowd	جمع من الناس
twenty	عشرون
pieces of gold	قطع من الذهب
pied piper	عازف المزمار

الكلمات الرئيسية

music	موسيقى
playing	يلعب
river	نهر
greedy	طمّاع
money	مال
suffer	عانى
children	أطفال
danced	رقص
sang	غنّى
rhythm	نغم/ إيقاع
tune	لحن
hill	تل
spell	سحر

يعود أصل أسطورة ال ـ بيد پايپرالى الأحداث التي وقعت في مدينةِ هامِلن في المانيا.
ويعود تاريخ هذه القصة الى سنة ١٢٨٦.
لِغرض الحصول على معلومات أكثر فان مدينة هامِلن لها موقع ممتاز
على الشبكةبالّانكليزية: http://www.hameln.com/englis

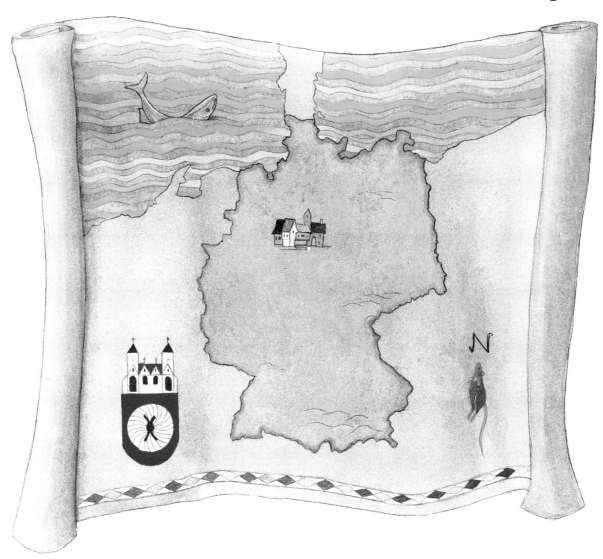

The legend of the Pied Piper originates from events that took place
in the town of Hameln in Germany. The story dates back to 1284.
If you would like more information the town of Hameln has an
excellent website in English: http://www.hameln.com/englis

If you've enjoyed this bilingual story in Arabic & English look out for other
Mantra titles in Arabic & English

Folk stories in Mantra's World Tales Series

Buri and the Marrow- an Indian folk story
Buskers of Bremen - adapted from the Brothers Grimm
Don't Cry Sly - adapted from Aesop's Fables
Dragon's Tears - a Chinese folk story
The Giant Turnip - a Russian folk story
Goldilocks and the Three Bears
Jack and the Beanstalk - an English folk story
Not Again Red Riding Hood
The Pied Piper - a German legend
Three Billy Goats Gruff - a Scandinavian folk story

Myths and Legends in Mantra's World Heritage Series

Beowulf - an Anglo Saxon Epic
The Children of Lir - a Celtic Myth
Hanuman's Challenge - an Indian Myth
Pandora's Box - a Greek Myth

Mantra's Contemporary Story Series

Alfie's Angels
Flash Bang Wheee!
Lima's Red Hot Chilli
Mei Ling's Hiccups
Sam's First Day
Samira's Eid
The Swirling Hijaab
That's My Mum
The Wibbly Wobbly Tooth

Mantra's Classic Story Series

Handa's Surprise
Splash!
The Very Hungry Caterpillar
Walking Through the Jungle
We're going on a Bear Hunt
What shall we do with the Boo Hoo Baby?

Many of the above books are also available on audio CD. To see the full range of Mantra's resources
do visit our website on www.mantralingua.com

The books on this page have been Pen enabled.
Please touch the Pen to the left hand corner of the page for further information on language availability
or visit
www.mantralingua.com

TalkingPEN™

علي بابا والاربعين حرامي

Ali Baba
and the *Forty Thieves*

Enebor Attard
Richard Holland

Arabic & English

Неужели опять,
Красная Шапочка!

Not Again, Red Riding Hood!
Kate Clynes & Louise Daykin

Ricitos de Oro y los tres ositos
Goldilocks and the Three Bears

Kate Clynes
Louise Daykin

Spanish & English

LA PETITE POULE ROUGE ET LES GRAINS DE BLE
The Little Red Hen and the *Grains of Wheat*

L. R. Hen
Jago

LION FABLES
by JAN ORMEROD

三隻山羊加菲

The Three Billy Goats Gruff

Henriette Barkow
Illustrated by Richard Johnson

Chinese & English

اللفتة العملاقة
The Giant Turnip

Adapted by Henriette Barkow
Illustrated by Richard Johnson

Arabic & English

Beowulf

Adapted by Henriette Barkow
Illustrated by Alan Down

German & English

The Children of Lir

Dawn Casey & Diana Mayo

흔들 근들 이
THE WIBBLY WOBBLY TOOTH
David Mills & Julia Crouth

Korean & English